HISTORY OF ARMENIA

Moses of Chorene

Translated by: B.P. Pratten

Edited by: D.P. Curtin

Translated by B.P. Pratten. From Ante-Nicene Fathers, Vol. 8. Edited by Alexander Roberts, James Donaldson, and A. Cleveland Coxe. (Buffalo, NY: Christian Literature Publishing Co., 1886.)

Library of Congress Cataloging-in-Publication Data

I. Reign of Abgar; Armenia becomes completely tributary to the Romans; war with Herod's troops; his brother's son, Joseph, is killed.

Abgar, son of Archam, ascends the throne in the twentieth year of Archavir, king of the Persians. This Abgar was called Avak-air (great man), on account of his great gentleness and wisdom, and also on account of his size. Not being able to pronounce well, the Greeks and the Syrians called him *Abgar*. In the second year of his reign, all the districts of Armenia become tributary to the Romans. A command is given by the Emperor Augustus, as we are told in the Gospel of St. Luke, to number all the people in every part. Roman commissioners, sent for that purpose into Armenia, carried there the statue of the Emperor Augustus, and set it up in all the temples. At this very time, our Saviour Jesus Christ, the Son of God, came into the world.

At the same period there was trouble between Abgar and Herod: for Herod wished that his statue should be erected near to that of Cæsar in the temples of Armenia. Abgar withstood this claim. Moreover, Herod was but seeking a pretext to attack Abgar: he sent an army of Thracians and Germans to make an incursion into the country of the Persians, with orders to pass through the territories of Abgar. But Abgar, far from submitting to this, resisted, saying that the emperor's command was to march the troops into Persia through the desert. Herod, indignant, and unable to act by himself, overwhelmed with troubles, as a punishment for his wicked conduct towards Christ, as Josephus relates, sent his nephew to whom he had given his daughter, who had been married in the first instance to Phéror, his brother. Herod's lieutenant, at the head of a considerable army, hastened to reach Mesopotamia, met Abgar at the camp in the province of Pouknan, fell in the combat, and his troops were put to flight. Soon afterwards, Herod died: Archelaus, his son, was appointed by Augustus ethnarch of Judæa.

II. Founding of the town of Edessa; brief account of the race of our illuminator.

A little while afterwards, Augustus dies, and Tiberius becomes emperor of the Romans in his stead. Germanicus, having become Cæsar, dragging in his train the princes of the kingdom of Archavir and of Abgar, celebrates a triumph in respect of the war waged with them, in which these princes had killed Herod's nephew. Abgar, indignant, forms plans of revolt and prepares himself for combat. He builds a town on the ground occupied by the Armenian army of observation, where previously the Euphrates had been defended against the attempts of Cassius: this new town is called Edessa. Abgar removed to it his court, which was at Medzpine, all his gods, Naboc, Bel, Patnicagh, and Tarata, the books of the schools attached to the temples, and even the royal archives.

After this, Archavir being dead, Ardachès, his son, reigns over the Persians. Though it is not in the order of the history with respect to time, nor even the order according to which we have begun these annals, yet, as we are treating of descendants of the king Archavir, even of the blood of Ardachès his son, we will, to do honour to these princes, place them, by anticipating the time, near to Ardachès, in order that the reader may know that they are of the same race, of the race of the brave Archag; then we will indicate the time of the arrival of their fathers in Armenia, the Garenians and the Sourenians, from whom St. Gregory and the Gamsarians are descended, when, following the order of events, we come to the reign of the king under whom they appeared.

Abgar did not succeed in his plans of revolt; for, troubles having arisen among his relatives in the Persian kingdom, he set out at the head of an army to allay and bring to an end the dissension.

III. Abgar comes into the East, maintains Ardachès upon the throne of Persia; reconciles his brothers from whom our illuminator and his relations are descended.

Abgar, having gone to the East, finds on the throne of Persia Ardachès, son of Archavir, and the brothers of Ardachès contending against him: for this prince thought to reign over them in his posterity, and they would not consent to it. Ardachès therefore hems them in on all sides, hangs the sword of death over their heads; distractions and dissension were between their troops and their other relations and allies: for King Archavir had three sons and one daughter; the first of these sons was King Ardachès himself, the second Garene, the third Sourene; their sister, named Gochm, was wife of the general of all the Ariks, a general chosen by their father Archavir.

Abgar prevails on the sons of Archavir to make peace; he arranges between them the conditions and stipulations: Ardachès is to reign with his posterity as he proposed, and his brothers are to be called Bahlav, from the name of their town and their vast and fertile country, so that their satrapies shall be the first, higher in rank than all the satrapies of Persia, as being truly a race of kings. Treaties and oaths stipulated that in case of the extinction of male children of Ardachès, his brothers should come to the throne; after the reigning race of Ardachès, his brothers are divided into three races named thus: the race of Garene Bahlav, the race of Sourene Bahlav, and the race of their sister, the race of Asbahabied Bahlav, a race thus called from the name of the domain of her husband.

St. Gregory is said to have sprung from the race Sourene Bahlav, and the Gamsarians from the race Garene Bahlav. We will relate in the sequel the circumstances of the coming of these personages, only mentioning their names here in connection with Ardachès, in order that you may know that these great races are indeed the blood of Vagharchag, that is to say, the posterity of the great Archag, brother of Vagharchag.

Everything being thus arranged, Abgar takes with him the letter of the treaties, and returns to his dominions; not in perfect health, but a prey to severe suffering.

IV. Abgar returns from the east; he gives help to Aretas in a war against Herod the Tetrarch.

When Abgar had returned from the East, he learned that the Romans suspected him of having gone there to raise troops. He therefore made the Roman commissioners acquainted with the reasons of his journey to Persia, as well as the treaty concluded between Ardachès and his brothers; but no credence was given to his statement: for he was accused by his enemies Pilate, Herod the tetrarch, Lysanias and Philip. Abgar having returned to his city Edessa leagued himself with Aretas, king of Petra, and gave him some auxiliary troops under the command of Khosran Ardzrouni, to make war upon Herod. Herod had in the first instance married the daughter of Aretas, then had repudiated her, and thereupon taken Herodias, even in her husband's lifetime, a circumstance in connection with which he had had John the Baptist put to death. Consequently there was war between Herod and Aretas on account of the wrong done the daughter of Aretas. Being sharply attacked, Herod's troops were defeated, thanks to the help of the brave Armenians; as if, by divine providence, vengeance was taken for the death of John the Baptist.

V. Abgar sends princes to Marinus; these deputies see our Saviour Christ; beginning of the conversion of Abgar.

At this period Marinus, son of Storoge, was raised by the emperor to the government of Phœnicia, Palestine, Syria, and Mesopotamia. Abgar sent to him two of his principal officers, Mar-Ihap prince of Aghtznik, and Chamchacram chief of the house of the Abahouni, as well as Anan his confidant. The envoys proceed to the town of Petkoupine to make known to Marinus the reasons of Abgar's journey to the East, showing him the treaty concluded between Ardachès and his brothers, and at the same time to call upon Marinus for his support. The deputies found the Roman governor at Eleutheropolis; he received them with friendship and distinction, and gave this answer to Abgar: Fear nothing from the emperor on that account, provided you take good care to pay the tribute regularly.

On their return, the Armenian deputies went to Jerusalem to see our Saviour the Christ, being attracted by the report of His miracles. Having themselves become eye-witnesses of these wonders, they related them to Abgar. This prince, seized with admiration, believed truly that Jesus was indeed the Son of God, and said: These wonders are not those of a man, but of a God. No, there is no one among men who can raise the dead: God alone has this power. Abgar felt in his whole body certain acute pains which he had got in Persia, more than seven years before; from men he had received no remedy for his sufferings; Abgar sent a letter of entreaty to Jesus: he prayed Him to come and cure him of his pains. Here is this letter:—

VI. Abgar's letter to the Saviour Jesus Christ.

Abgar, son of Archam, prince of the land, to Jesus, Saviour and Benefactor of men, who has appeared in the country of Jerusalem, greeting:—

I have heard of You, and of the cures wrought by Your hands, without remedies, without herbs: for, as it is said, You make the blind to see, the lame to walk, the lepers to be healed; You drive out unclean spirits, You cure unhappy beings afflicted with prolonged and inveterate diseases; You even raise the dead. As I have heard of all these wonders wrought by You, I have concluded from them either that You are God, come down from heaven to do such great things, or that You are the Son of God, working as You do these miracles. Therefore have I written to You, praying You to condescend to come to me and cure me of the complaints with which I am afflicted. I have heard also that the Jews murmur against You and wish to deliver You up to torments: I have a city small but pleasant, it would be sufficient for us both.

The messengers, the bearers of this letter, met Jesus at Jerusalem, a fact confirmed by these words of the Gospel: Some from among the heathen came to find Jesus, but those who heard them, not daring to tell Jesus what they had heard, told it to Philip and Andrew, who repeated it all to their Master.

The Saviour did not then accept the invitation given to Him, but He thought fit to honour Abgar with an answer in these words:—

VII. Answer to Abgar's letter, which the apostle Thomas wrote to this prince by command of the Saviour.

Blessed is he who believes in me without having seen me! For it is written of me: 'Those who see me will not believe in me, and those who do not see me will believe and live.' As to what you have written asking me to come to you, I must accomplish here all that for which I have been sent; and, when I shall have accomplished it all, I shall ascend to Him who sent me; and when I shall go away I will send one of my disciples, who will cure your diseases, and give life to you and to all those who are with you. Anan, Abgar's courier, brought him this letter, as well as the portrait of the Saviour, a picture which is still to be found at this day in the city of Edessa.

VIII. Preaching of the apostle Thaddæus at Edessa; copy of five letters.

After the ascension of our Saviour, the Apostle Thomas, one of the twelve, sent one of the seventy-six disciples, Thaddæus, to the city of Edessa to heal Abgar and to preach the Gospel, according to the word of the Lord. Thaddæus came to the house of Tobias, a Jewish prince, who is said to have been of the race of the Pacradouni. Tobias, having left Archam, did not abjure Judaism with the rest of his relatives, but followed its laws up to the moment when he believed in Christ. Soon the name of Thaddæus spreads through the whole town. Abgar, on learning of his arrival, said: This is indeed he concerning whom Jesus wrote to me; and immediately Abgar sent for the apostle. When Thaddæus entered, a marvellous appearance presented itself to the eyes of Abgar in the countenance of the apostle; the king having risen from his throne, fell on his face to the earth, and prostrated himself before Thaddæus. This spectacle greatly surprised all the princes who were present, for they were ignorant of the fact of the vision. Are you really, said Abgar to Thaddæus, are you the disciple of the ever-blessed Jesus? Are you he whom He promised to send to me, and can you heal my maladies? Yes, answered Thaddæus; if you believe in Jesus Christ, the Son of God, the desires of your heart shall be granted. I have believed in Jesus, said Abgar, I have believed in His Father; therefore I wished to go at the head of my troops to destroy the Jews who have crucified Jesus, had I not been prevented by reason of the power of the Romans.

Thenceforth Thaddæus began to preach the Gospel to the king and his town; laying his hands upon Abgar, he cured him; he cured also a man with gout, Abdu, a prince of the town, much honoured in all the king's house. He also healed all the sick and infirm people in the town, and all believed in Jesus Christ. Abgar was baptized, and all the town with him, and the temples of the false gods were closed, and all the statues of idols that were placed on the altars and columns were hidden by being covered with reeds. Abgar did not compel any one to embrace the faith yet from day to day the number of the believers was multiplied.

The Apostle Thaddæus baptizes a manufacturer of silk head-dresses, called Attæus, consecrates him, appoints him *to minister* at Edessa, and leaves him with the king instead of himself. Thaddæus, after having received letters patent from Abgar, who wished that all should listen to the Gospel of Christ, went to find Sanadroug, son of Abgar's sister, whom this prince had appointed over the country and over the army. Abgar was pleased to write to the Emperor Tiberius a letter in these words:—

Abgar's letter to Tiberius

Abgar, king of Armenia, to my Lord Tiberius, emperor of the Romans, greeting:—

I know that nothing is unknown to your Majesty, but, as your friend, I would make you better acquainted with the facts by writing. The Jews who dwell in the cantons of Palestine have crucified Jesus: Jesus without sin, Jesus after so many acts of kindness, so many wonders and miracles wrought for their good, even to the raising of the dead. Be assured that these are not the effects of the power of a simple mortal, but of God. During the time that they were crucifying Him, the sun was darkened, the earth was moved, shaken; Jesus Himself, three days afterwards, rose from the dead and appeared to many. Now, everywhere, His name alone, invoked by His disciples, produces the greatest miracles: what has happened to myself is the most evident proof of it. Your august Majesty knows henceforth what ought to be done in future with respect to the Jewish nation, which has committed this crime; your Majesty knows whether a command should not be published through the whole universe to worship Christ as the true God. Safety and health.

Answer from Tiberius to Abgar's letter

Tiberius, emperor of the Romans, to Abgar, king of the Armenians, greeting:—

Your kind letter has been read to me, and I wish that thanks should be given to you from me. Though we had already heard several persons relate these facts, Pilate has officially informed us of the miracles of Jesus. He has certified to us that after His resurrection from the dead He was acknowledged by many to be God. Therefore I myself also wished to do what you propose; but, as it is the custom of the Romans not to admit a god merely by the command of the sovereign, but only when the admission has been discussed and examined in full senate, I proposed the affair to the senate, and they rejected it with contempt, doubtless because it had not been considered by them first. But we have commanded all those whom Jesus suits, to receive him among the gods. We have threatened with death any one who shall speak evil of the Christians. As to the Jewish nation which has dared to crucify Jesus, who, as I hear, far from deserving the cross and death, was worthy of honour, worthy of the adoration of men— when I am free from the war with rebellious Spain, I will examine into the matter, and will treat the Jews as they deserve.

Abgar writes another letter to Tiberius

Abgar, king of the Armenians, to my lord Tiberius, emperor of the Romans, greeting:—

I have received the letter written from your august Majesty, and I have applauded the commands which have emanated from your wisdom. If you will not be angry with me, I will say that the conduct of the senate is extremely ridiculous and absurd: for, according to the senators, it is after the examination and by the suffrages of men that divinity may be ascribed. Thus, then, if God does not suit man, He cannot be God, since God is to be judged and justified by man. It will no doubt seem just to my lord and master to send another governor to Jerusalem in the place of Pilate, who ought to be ignominiously driven from the powerful post in which you placed him; for he has done the will of the Jews: he has crucified Christ unjustly, without your order. That you may enjoy health is my desire.

Abgar, having written this letter, placed a copy of it, with copies of the other letters, in his archives. He wrote also to the young Nerseh, king of Assyria, at Babylon:—

Abgar's letter to Nerseh

Abgar, king of the Armenians, to my son Nerseh, greeting:—

I have received your letter and acknowledgments. I have released Beroze from his chains, and have pardoned his offenses: if this pleases you, give him the government of Nineveh. But as to what you write to me about sending you the physician who works miracles and preaches another God superior to fire and water, that you may see and hear him, I say to you: he was not a physician according to the art of men; he was a disciple of the Son of God, Creator of fire and water: he has been appointed and sent to the countries of Armenia. But one of his principal companions, named Simon, is sent into the countries of Persia. Seek for him, and you will hear him, you as well as your father Ardachès. He will heal all your diseases and will show you the way of life.

Abgar's letter to Ardachès

Abgar wrote also to Ardachès, king of the Persians, the following letter:—

Abgar, king of the Armenians, to Ardachès my brother, king of the Persians, greeting:—

I know that you have heard of Jesus Christ the Son of God, whom the Jews have crucified, Jesus who was raised from the dead, and has sent His disciples through all the world to instruct men. One of His chief disciples, named Simon, is in your Majesty's territories. Seek for him, and you will find him, and he will cure you of all your maladies, and will show you the way of life, and you will believe in his words, you, and your brothers, and all those who willingly obey you. It is very pleasant to me to think that my relations in the flesh will be also my relations, my friends, in the spirit.

Abgar had not yet received answers to these letters when he died, having reigned thirty-eight years.

IX. Martyrdom of our apostles.

After the death of Abgar, the kingdom of Armenia was divided between two: Ananoun, Abgar's son, reigned at Edessa, and his sister's son, Sanadroug, in Armenia. What took place in their time has been previously told by others: the apostle's arrival in Armenia, the conversion of Sanadroug and his apostasy for fear of the Armenian satraps, and the martyrdom of the apostle and his companions in the canton of Chavarchan, now called Ardaz, and the stone opening to receive the body of the apostle, and the removal of this body by his disciples, his burial in the plain, and the martyrdom of the king's daughter, Santoukhd, near the road, and the apparition of the remains of the two saints, and their removal to the rocks— all circumstances related by others, as we have said, a long time before us: we have not thought it important to repeat them here. In the same way also what is related of the martyrdom at Edessa of Attæus, a disciple of the apostle, a martyrdom ordered by Abgar's son, has been told by others before us.

The prince who reigned after the death of his father, did not inherit his father's virtues: he opened the temples of the idols, and embraced the religion of the heathen. He sent word to Attæus: Make me a head-dress of cloth interwoven with gold, like those you formerly used to make for my father. He received this answer from Attæus: My hands shall not make a head-dress for an unworthy prince, who does not worship Christ the living God.

Immediately the king ordered one of his armed men to cut off Attæus' feet. The soldier went, and, seeing the holy man seated in the chair of the teacher, cut off his legs with his sword, and immediately the saint gave up the ghost. We mention this cursorily, as a fact related by others a long while ago. There came then into Armenia the Apostle Bartholomew, who suffered martyrdom among us in the town of Arepan. As to Simon, who was sent unto Persia, I cannot relate with certainty what he did, nor where he suffered martyrdom. It is said that one Simon, an apostle, was martyred at Veriospore. Is this true, or why did the saint come to this place? I do not know; I have only mentioned this circumstance that you may know I spare no pains to tell you all that is necessary.

X. Reign of Sanadroug; murder of Abgar's children; the princess Helena.

Sanadroug, being on the throne, raises troops with the help of the brave Pacradouni and Ardzrouni, who had exalted him, and goes to wage war upon the children of Abgar, to make him self master of the whole kingdom. Whilst Sanadroug was occupied with these affairs, as if by an effect of divine providence vengeance was taken for the death of Attæus; for a marble column which the son of Abgar was having erected at Edessa, on the summit of his palace, while he was underneath to direct the work, escaped from the hands of the workmen, fell upon him and crushed his feet.

Immediately there came a message from the inhabitants of the town, asking Sanadroug for a treaty by which he should engage not to disturb them in the exercise of the Christian religion, in consideration of which, they would give up the town and the king's treasures. Sanadroug promised, but in the end violated his oath. Sanadroug put all the children of the house of Abgar to the edge of the sword, with the exception of the daughters, whom he withdrew from the town to place them in the canton of Hachdiank. As to the first of Abgar's wives, named Helena, he sent her to his town at Kharan, and left to her the sovereignty of the whole of Mesopotamia, in remembrance of the benefits he had received from Abgar by Helena's means.

Helena, pious like her husband Abgar, did not wish to live in the midst of idolaters; she went away to Jerusalem in the time of Claudius, during the famine which Agabus had predicted; with all her treasures she bought in Egypt an immense quantity of grain, which she distributed among the poor, a fact to which Josephus testifies. Helena's tomb, a truly remarkable one, is still to be seen before the gate of Jerusalem.

XI. Restoration of the town of Medzpine; name of Sanadroug; his death.

Of all Sanadroug's doings and actions, we judge none worthy of remembrance except the building of the town of Medzpine; for, this town having been shaken by an earthquake, Sanadroug pulled it down, rebuilt it more magnificently, and surrounded it with double walls and ramparts. Sanadroug caused to be erected in the middle of the town his statue holding in his hand a single piece of money, which signifies: All my treasures have been used in building the town, and no more than this single piece of money is left to me.

But why was this prince called Sanadroug? We will tell you: Because Abgar's sister, Otæa, while travelling in Armenia in the winter, was assailed by a whirlwind of snow in the Gortouk mountains; the tempest separated them all, so that none of them knew where his companion had been driven. The prince's nurse, Sanod, sister of Piourad Pacradouni, wife of Khosran Ardzrouni, having taken the royal infant, for Sanadroug was still in the cradle, laid him upon her bosom, and remained with him under the snow three days and three nights. Legend has taken possession of this circumstance: it relates that an animal, a new species, wonderful, of great whiteness, sent by the gods, guarded the child. But so far as we have been informed, this is the fact: a white dog, which was among the men sent in search, found the child and his nurse; the prince was therefore called Sanadroug, a name taken from his nurse's name (and from the Armenian name, *dourk*, a gift), as if to signify the gift of Sanod.

Sanadroug, having ascended the throne in the twelfth year of Ardachès, king of the Persians, and having lived thirty years, died as he was hunting, from an arrow which pierced his bowels, as if in punishment of the torments which he had made his holy daughter suffer. Gheroupna, son of the scribe Apchatar, collected all these facts, happening in the time of Abgar and Sanadroug, and placed them in the archives of Edessa.